Redford Township District Library
25320 West Six Mile Road
Redford, MI 48240

www.redford.lib.mi.us

Hours:

Mon–Thur 10–8:30
Fri–Sat 10–5
Sunday (School Year) 12–5

39009000007746

D1258165

WHY SHOULD I WASH MY HAIR?
✦ and other questions about healthy skin

and hair ✦

Louise Spilsbury

Heinemann Library
Chicago, Illinois

Customer Service 888-454-2279

Visit our website at www.heinemannlibrary.com

Designed by David Poole and Tokay Interactive Ltd
Illustrations by Kamae Design Ltd
Originated by Ambassador Litho Ltd
Printed in China by Wing King Tong

07 06 05 04 03
10 9 8 7 6 5 4 3 2 1

Library of Congress Cataloging-in-Publication Data
Spilsbury, Louise.
  Why should I wash my hair? : and other questions about healthy skin
and hair / Louise Spilsbury.
      v. cm. -- (Body matters)
Includes bibliographical references and index.
Contents: Why is healthy skin important? -- Why should I care for my
hair? -- Why should I take a shower or bath? -- How often should I wash
my hair? -- Why does my hair itch? -- Why should I brush my hair? -- Why
should I wear sunscreen? -- Why do I get pimples? -- Why do I get a
skin rash? -- How can I soothe sore skin? -- Amazing facts about skin
and hair.
  ISBN 1-4034-4685-7 (HC)
  1. Skin--Juvenile literature. 2. Hair--Juvenile literature. 3.
Skin--Care and hygiene--Juvenile literature. 4. Hair--Care and
hygiene--Juvenile literature. [1. Skin. 2. Hair. 3. Skin--Care and
hygiene. 4. Hair--Care and hygiene.] I. Title. II. Series.
  QP88.5.S66 2003
  612.7'9--dc21
                        2003004982

Acknowledgments
The author and publishers are grateful to the following for permission to reproduce copyright material:
pp. 4, 8, 24 Getty Images/Taxi; pp. 5, 14, 18, 19, 26 Science Photo Library; pp. 7, 23 Getty Images/Imagebank; pp. 10, 11, 12, 15, 17, 21, 28 Tudor Photography; p. 13 Bubbles/Jennie Woodcock; p. 16 Getty Images/Liz Eddison; p. 20 Bubbles/Nancy Nev; p. 22 Bubbles/Angela Hampton; p. 25 Bubbles/Paul A. Souders; p. 27 Bubbles/Lester V. Bergman.

Cover photograph by Tudor Photography.

Some words are shown in bold, **like this.** You can find out what they mean by looking in the glossary.

CONTENTS

WHY IS HEALTHY SKIN IMPORTANT?

You may not think of your skin as having much to do—it just covers your body. In fact, skin is a vitally important body part, like your heart or brain, and you should take care of it.

Skin protection

Skin is like your body's armor. It may feel soft, but skin works very hard, protecting your insides from dirt and dust, bumps and blows, wind and rain, and **germs.** Although germs can get into your body through your mouth and nose, the only way they can get through your skin is if you have a cut in it.

Your skin is like a waterproof coat—it stops water from getting into and out of your body. The organs inside your body need just the right amount of moisture to work well. Your skin keeps them from getting too wet or too dry.

4

Hot and cold

Your skin helps keep your body at a healthy
temperature. On a cold day, the hairs on your
skin stand up, trapping a layer of warm air
around you. Small **blood vessels** under the skin,
called capillaries, get thinner. This keeps them
away from the skin's surface so they can hold on
to their warmth. When it is hot, the hairs lie flat,
and the capillaries bring warm blood to the
skin's surface to release some of their heat.

A touchy subject?

Your skin also provides you with your sense of
touch. It lets you feel whether something is hard
or soft, or hot or cold. **Nerve endings** just
beneath the surface of your skin send messages
to your brain about everything that you touch.

When hair on your
skin stands up to
trap warmth, we call
it goosebumps.

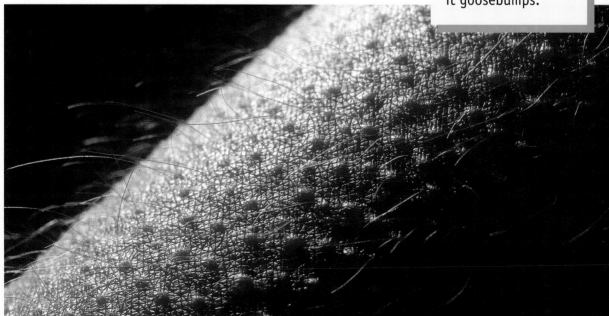

How does skin work?

Your skin is made up of three layers. The outside layer—the epidermis—is always changing. New **cells** made at the bottom slowly work their way to the top, filling up with a tough substance called **keratin** as they go. They die as they reach the top. There, they form the skin's surface.

The middle layer—the dermis—contains **nerve endings, blood vessels,** and **glands.** Blood vessels bring food and **oxygen** to the cells. Glands make oil and sweat.

The bottom layer—called the subcutaneous layer—is mostly fat. It helps keep you warm and acts as a cushion, absorbing the shock when you bump your skin.

Your skin is not as simple as it looks!

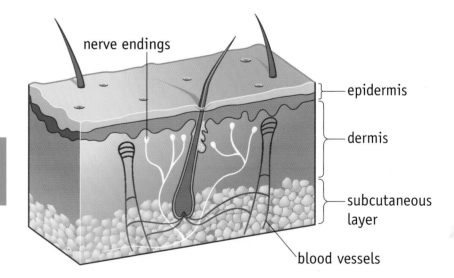

nerve endings

epidermis

dermis

subcutaneous layer

blood vessels

WHY SHOULD I CARE FOR MY HAIR?

You should take care of the hair on your head because it has a very important job to do. It helps to keep your brain at a steady temperature. The brain is one of the most important parts in your body—it controls everything you think, feel and do—and it needs to be at a steady temperature to work at its best.

On a cold day, your hair helps keep your head warm. On a hot day, it protects your head from some of the sun's heat. Your hair also provides some cushioning when you bump your head, helping to keep your brain from being hurt.

Your hair is also important because it is a part of who you are. If you are asked to describe someone, chances are that one of the first things you will describe is his or her hair color and style.

SKIN AND HAIR COLOR

A person's skin color is often linked to his or her hair color because skin and hair color are decided by the amount of melanin a person makes. People with blond or red hair make less melanin, so they also have light skin. People with dark skin make more melanin, so they usually have dark hair.

Why do people have different colored hair?

The thing that decides whether you have blond, brown, red, or black hair is the amount of **melanin** your body makes. Melanin is a substance that colors skin and hair. **Cells** in the epidermis make melanin. They color hair as it grows. The more melanin you make, the darker your hair is. As you get older, you make less melanin. That is why elderly people have gray or white hair.

You **inherit** the kind of hair you have from your parents.

How does hair grow?

You have hair all over your body, and all of it grows in the same way—from roots.
A root is a patch of cells that form **keratin,** a substance that makes your hair strong. Each root is inside a **follicle.** At the bottom of the follicles, there are tiny **blood vessels** that supply the root with food.

The root is the only part of a hair that is alive. It makes a strand of hair grow out of a **pore** (tiny hole) in the skin. The hair that you can see is dead. It is made up of dead cells of keratin. After a while, the strand of hair falls out, and the root makes a new one to replace it.

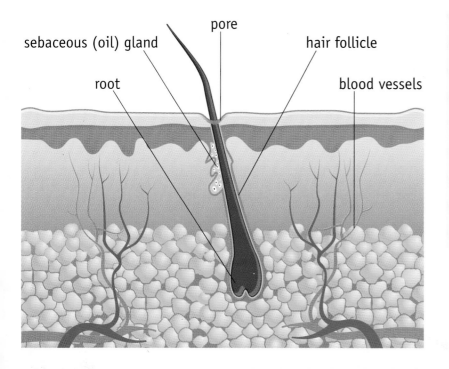

sebaceous (oil) gland

pore

hair follicle

root

blood vessels

Near each hair follicle is a **sebaceous gland,** which makes a kind of oil called sebum. This oil helps make your hair shine and also makes it a bit waterproof.

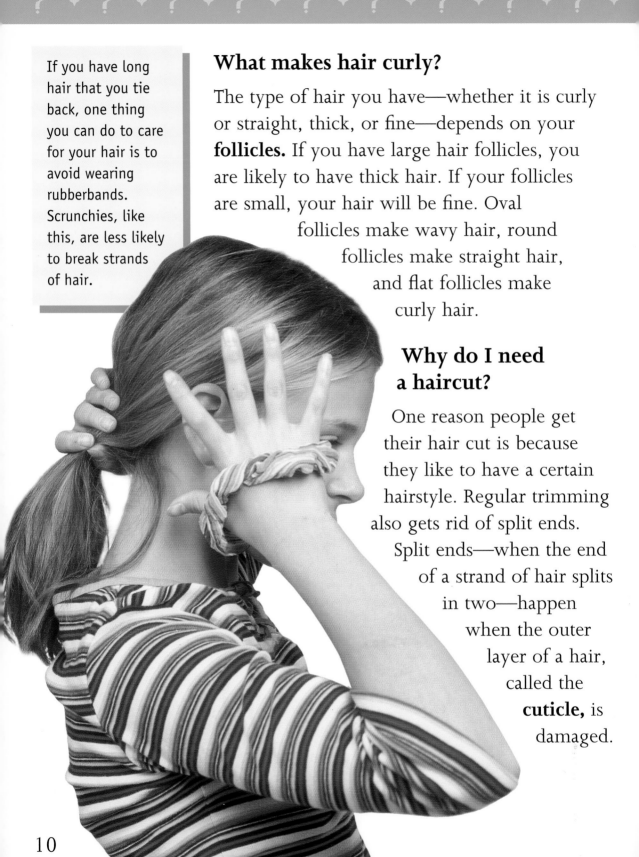

If you have long hair that you tie back, one thing you can do to care for your hair is to avoid wearing rubberbands. Scrunchies, like this, are less likely to break strands of hair.

What makes hair curly?

The type of hair you have—whether it is curly or straight, thick, or fine—depends on your **follicles.** If you have large hair follicles, you are likely to have thick hair. If your follicles are small, your hair will be fine. Oval follicles make wavy hair, round follicles make straight hair, and flat follicles make curly hair.

Why do I need a haircut?

One reason people get their hair cut is because they like to have a certain hairstyle. Regular trimming also gets rid of split ends. Split ends—when the end of a strand of hair splits in two—happen when the outer layer of a hair, called the **cuticle,** is damaged.

10

WHY SHOULD I TAKE A SHOWER OR BATH?

You need to take showers or baths because an important part of taking care of your skin is keeping it clean. One of your skin's most important jobs is to protect your insides from **germs.** You need to help your skin to do its job by washing off dust, dirt, and stale sweat, which can carry germs.

What is sweat?

When you get hot, your sweat **glands** make sweat—a kind of salty water. The sweat leaves your body through tiny holes in your skin, called **pores.** As sweat dries in the air, it cools you down. Some sweat stays on your skin, and **bacteria** start to grow on it. This is what makes sweat smell. If these bacteria get into your body, they can make you ill.

When you wash, you also rub off the old, dead skin **cells** that build up on your skin's surface.

11

Why do I need to use soap?

Believe it or not, water by itself is not much use for cleaning. Water has a property called surface tension, which makes it run off surfaces. This means that it is hard for water to stick to surfaces you want to clean, such as your skin. By using soap with water, you can reduce the water's surface tension. Using warm water also helps because the hotter the water is, the less surface tension it has.

Soap helps water spread out and wet your skin properly. Soap also attaches itself to any bits of dust or dirt so that when you rinse off the soap, the dirt gets washed away, too.

When a drop of water lands on your skin, it forms a bead shape and does not soak in. When you add soap, the water spreads and wets your skin to wash away dirt and **germs.**

What soap should I use?

For most people, it does not matter what kind of soap they use. If you have sensitive skin—skin that is easily irritated—you should avoid soaps that have a lot of perfume in them. Try to buy pure soaps or those that are specially designed for people with sensitive skin.

WAYS OF WASHING

Do not use water that is very hot when you take a shower or bath because it can scald (burn) your skin. Cold water does not clean well, so use warm water. Germs grow well in damp places, so dry yourself thoroughly with a clean towel after washing. Dry between your toes, too—this helps prevent **athlete's foot.**

Showers are a good way to wash because you can rinse off dirt more easily. Showers also use less water than baths, and it is good to save water when you can.

WHY SHOULD I WASH MY HAIR?

There are no hard and fast rules about washing your hair. Most young people wash their hair about two or three times a week, or when it feels dirty. You need to wash it more often if you exercise a lot, or if it is very hot and you sweat a lot.

Why does my hair need washing?

You need to wash your hair to keep it clean.

This picture shows hair coming out of a **scalp.** At the bottom of each strand, you can see dead skin **cells,** which look like flakes. When you wash your hair, you wash these off.

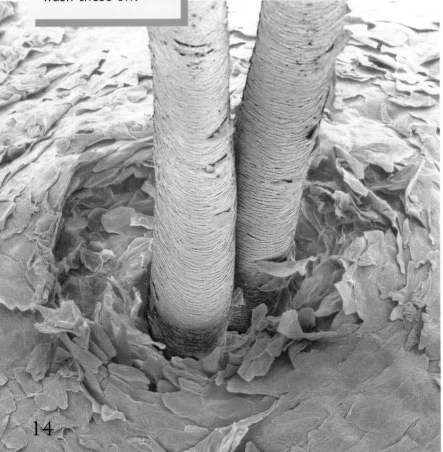

Some people find that their hair feels oily when it needs washing because their **sebaceous glands** have made too much oil. Dirt and dust collect on your hair, just as they do on your clothes and skin, so you need to wash those off, too.

Can you wash your hair too often?

Although it is good to wash your hair regularly, it is bad to wash it too often. When you use shampoo, you also wash off some of the natural oils that your skin produces to coat your hair as it grows. These oils are important because they keep the hair soft and waterproof.

WHY WASH HAIR AFTER SWIMMING?

You should always wash your hair after swimming. Swimming pools contain chemicals, such as chlorine, that can burn your hair if they stay on it for too long. Seawater is salty and dries your hair out, so make sure that you wash it out of your hair after swimming in the ocean.

When you wash your hair, use warm water and rub the shampoo in with your fingertips. Rinse your hair with clean water to get out all the shampoo.

Some people prefer to use natural shampoos. These are usually made from plants and do not contain the strong chemicals that some ordinary shampoos contain.

Why use shampoo?

Most people use shampoo to wash their hair for the same reason that they use soap to wash their skin. Because of surface tension, water is not very good at wetting or cleaning when used on its own. The oily layer on your hair is slightly waterproof, so the water just runs off it. The **detergents** in shampoo attach to the dirt and flakes of dead **cells** on your hair so that, when you rinse it, they wash away down the drain with the water.

WHAT IS IN SHAMPOO?

Most shampoos contain water; substances called foaming agents, which make bubbles when the shampoo is mixed with water; detergents to clean the hair; and perfumes to cover up the smell of the detergents.

Which shampoo should I use?

Try to use a shampoo that says "mild" or "gentle" on the label. Strong shampoos may contain more chemicals, which can damage your hair. If your hair feels oily, you may need to use a shampoo made especially for oily hair.

What is conditioner?

People sometimes use conditioner after washing their hair with shampoo. You usually spread a small amount of conditioner on your hair, leave it in for a minute, and then rinse it thoroughly with clean water. Conditioners help to make the surface of hair smooth, avoiding tangles and making long hair easier to brush.

After washing your hair, let it dry in the air if you can. If you have long hair, or you are in a hurry, you may have to use a hair dryer. Do not hold it too close or have it too hot, because heat can damage your hair.

WHY DOES MY HEAD ITCH?

Your head can itch for several reasons. You may be using the wrong kind of shampoo, or you may have a flaky **scalp.** This is called dandruff, and it happens when skin flakes because your scalp makes too much oil. You can cure dandruff by using a special shampoo. Another common reason for an itchy head is lice.

This photo makes a head louse look big. In fact, head lice are only 0.08 to 0.12 in. (2 to 3 mm) long.

What are head lice?

Head lice are very small insects that live in people's hair. They feed on tiny amounts of blood from the scalp, and their bites make your head itch. They lay tiny white eggs, called nits, on hairs near the scalp. Nits hatch after about a week. Head lice live for four or five weeks, and they can lay eggs from when they are about two weeks old.

How do you get head lice?

Some people think that you get head lice if your hair is dirty. In fact, head lice prefer clean hair because it is less oily for them when they feed. You get head lice from touching heads with someone who already has them. You can also get it by sharing hairbrushes, combs, helmets, hats, or scrunchies.

How can you get rid of them?

You can kill head lice by washing your hair with a special shampoo. Your whole family should treat their hair at the same time because chances are that other family members have them, too. After you have killed the live lice, you can use a special comb with narrow teeth to comb through your hair and pull out any remaining nits. If you put on a conditioner first, this makes it easier to comb through.

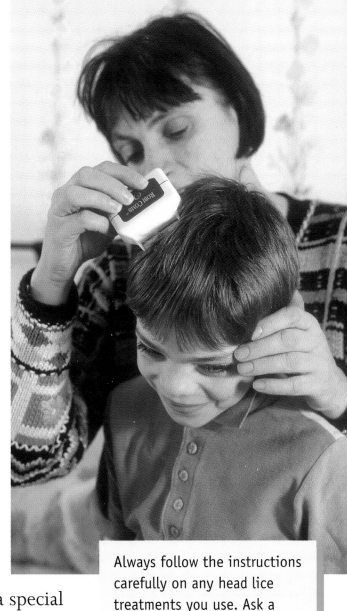

Always follow the instructions carefully on any head lice treatments you use. Ask a grown-up to help you.

WHY SHOULD I BRUSH MY HAIR?

The way you brush your hair and how often you brush it depend on the kind of hair you have. People with short hair may just run a comb through their hair once a day. Long hair gets tangled easily, however, so it needs to be brushed more thoroughly.

Some people with very curly hair wear braids so that their hair does not get tangled and does not need to be brushed.

What does brushing do?

Brushing hair gets rid of some of the dead skin **cells** and dirt that build up in your hair. It also helps to spread the oil produced by the **sebaceous glands** down the whole length of your hair. If you have head lice, combing your hair with a fine-toothed comb is an important step in getting rid of the lice.

TIPS FOR BRUSHING YOUR HAIR

- Choose a comb or brush that suits your hair. If you have tight, curly hair, use a wide-toothed comb.

- If you have oily hair, do not brush it too much. Doing so makes the sebaceous glands produce more oil, which makes your hair even oilier.

- Brush your hair before you wash it to reduce the number of tangles you get.

- Have your own brush or comb and try not to share it with anyone else. This avoids spreading **germs** and head lice. Clean your comb or brush regularly.

- Hair breaks easily when it is wet, so try not to brush it until it is dry—or use a wide-toothed comb.

Brush the ends of your hair first, and work your way up. This helps to get any tangles out and makes it less likely that you will damage your hair.

21

WHY SHOULD I WEAR SUNSCREEN?

Sunlight can damage your hair and your skin. It contains ultraviolet (UV) rays, which are very strong. They can burn your skin and hair and also cause a serious disease called skin cancer. On sunny days, you should always wear a hat to shade your hair and sunscreen to protect your skin.

People with light skin make less melanin than people with dark skin, so they have to be extra careful in the sun.

Why does my skin darken in the sun?

Have you noticed how your skin gets darker in the sun? This is because the skin tries to protect itself from harmful UV rays by making more **melanin.** The more melanin your skin makes, the darker your skin looks. You must still use sunscreen even if you have dark skin, but fair-skinned people get sunburned more easily.

Which sunscreen should I use?

Every bottle of sunscreen should have the lotion's SPF—sun protection factor—rating. The higher the SPF rating, the more protection the sunscreen provides. Choose one with an SPF rating of at least 15. Rub it all over the uncovered parts of your body, including your ears and feet! Reapply every two or three hours—more often if you are swimming or sweating a lot because this washes it off.

Other ways to protect your skin

You should also wear T-shirts and shorts or skirts made of tightly woven fabric, which help to block out the sun's rays; a hat with a wide brim, to protect your hair and the skin on your face and neck; and sunglasses, to protect the delicate skin around your eyes.

Even if you cover up and wear sunscreen, try to keep out of the sun during the hottest part of the day, between 11 A.M. and 3 P.M.

WHY DO I GET PIMPLES?

A lot of young people get pimples. Pimples do not form because you eat too many french fries or chocolate bars. They form when the **sebaceous glands** in your skin make too much oil.

How do pimples form?

Your sebaceous glands make oil to keep the outer layer of skin—the part that is made up of dead **cells**— smooth and soft. Sometimes these glands make too much oil. When the oil mixes with dead skin cells, it can form a plug over the **pores** in your skin. Whiteheads form when **bacteria** around a pore get trapped in it. The body makes pus to try to break down the bacteria.

The black stuff you see in a blackhead is not dirt—it is dried oil and skin cells. They turn black when they react with the air.

How can I stop pimples?

Everyone gets pimples sometimes, and you will not be able to make your body a pimple-free zone, whatever you do. You can help by cleaning your skin carefully, especially if you have had sunscreen, glitter, or face paint on it. Wash your face before you go to bed with a gentle soap and warm water. If your skin does not feel greasy in the morning, just rinse it with warm water. Washing too often with soap can take away the oils that your skin needs.

DON'T PICK ON ME!

The one thing you should not do is to pop or pick a pimple. This can make the pimple bigger and redder, make it feel sore, and damage the delicate skin on your face.

Face paints are fun, but make sure that you wash them off carefully before you go to bed.

WHY DO I HAVE A SKIN RASH?

A skin rash is when your skin looks red and blotchy. It may feel dry and itchy, too, or the skin may be raised in little blisters.

What causes a skin rash?

Many different things can cause a skin rash. You may have touched or eaten something that caused it, or maybe you used a different soap or dish **detergent** (if you help clean up after dinner). Sometimes people get a rash after being in the heat, touching certain plants, or getting stung by an insect. Illnesses or some **infections** can also cause rashes. Some people have **allergies** that affect their skin as well.

Eczema is a skin problem that causes itching and a red rash. It is often caused by certain foods or breathing in dust or other particles. You cannot catch eczema from touching someone who has it.

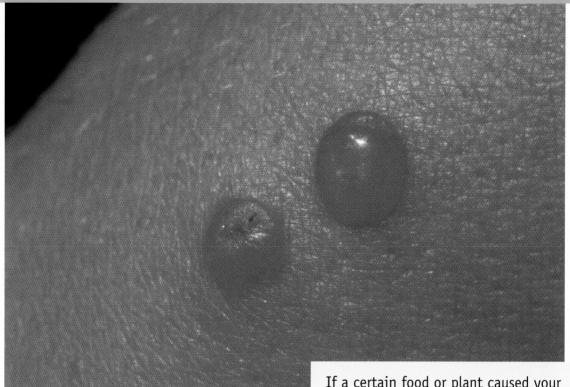

How can I get rid of a rash?

If you get a rash because of something you ate or touched, it should go away by itself quickly. If it does not, you should see a doctor. The doctor will give you some medicine to stop the rash. If the rash is caused by an allergy, a doctor can help you find out what you are allergic to and can give you medicine to help.

If a certain food or plant caused your rash, make sure you avoid it in the future. These blisters were caused by contact with oil from a poison ivy plant.

WHY CAN'T I SCRATCH A RASH?

Don't scratch a rash because it may make your skin sore and may also spread the rash. You can put on calamine lotion or hydrocortisone cream to stop the itch.

HOW CAN I SOOTHE SORE SKIN

Sometimes your skin can get sore. If you cut yourself, the most important thing to do is to wash the area with soap and warm water. Then put an **antiseptic** cream on the cut to prevent **infection.** If the cut is big or deep, you may need to see a doctor, who can close up the wound with a special bandage or stitches.

How can I soothe sunburn?

Put cool damp washcloths on the sunburn to lessen the burning feeling. Then soak in a bath of tepid (just warm) water, but do not use soap because this will make your skin sorer. Pat yourself dry gently instead of rubbing your skin. Use an aftersun cream or calamine or aloe lotion to help soothe the skin.

As long as you keep small cuts clean, it is better not to cover them because the air will help them heal. But even larger cuts that need to be covered do not have to stop you from being active.

AMAZING FACTS ABOUT SKIN AND HAIR

- There are about 5 million hairs on a human body, many of them so small that you can barely see them.

- The hairs on your head grow at a rate of about 0.2 inch (5 millimeters) every week.

- You lose between 50 and 100 hairs from your head every day.

- People with different colored hair have different numbers of hairs on their head! Redheads have about 80,000 hairs on their head, brown-haired and black-haired people have 100,000, and blonds have at least 120,000.

- The outer layer of your skin is made of **cells** that died days before.

- You have more hairs on your body than an ape! It is true—but the hair on your body is so short and fine that it is not so obvious.

GLOSSARY

allergy   when the body reacts to something harmless as though it were a germ

antiseptic   substance that destroys the germs that cause infections

athlete's foot   itchy skin on the foot

bacteria   tiny living things that can cause disease

blood vessel   tube that carries blood in the body

cell   smallest building block of living things

cuticle   outer layer of hair

detergent   substance that loosens and removes dirt

follicle   point from which a hair grows

germ   tiny living thing that can cause disease

gland   body part that makes substances, such as sweat and oil

infection   when germs get inside the body and cause disease

inherit   to take on traits, such as hair or eye color, from your parents

keratin   kind of hard protein

melanin   substance that colors skin and hair

nerve endings points in the skin that let you feel things, such as pain, heat and cold, and pressure

oxygen gas in the air that people need to breathe

pore tiny hole in the upper layer of the skin

scalp skin that covers the top of the head

sebaceous gland gland under the skin that makes a kind of oil, called sebum, that keeps skin and hair soft and waterproof

FURTHER READING

Brallier, Jess. *Hairy Science: All You Need Is Hair!* New York: Sterling, 1997.

Goode, Katherine. *Skin and Hair.* Farmington Hills, Mich.: Blackbirch Press, 2000.

Royston, Angela. *Healthy Hair.* Chicago: Heinemann Library, 2003.

Stewart, Alex. *Keeping Clean.* Danbury, Conn.: Scholastic Library, 2000.

Wingate, Philippa. *Hair.* Wilmington, Del.: Usborne, 2000.

INDEX